BIRDBOOK I

TOWNS, PARKS, GARDENS & WOODLAND

EDITED BY KIRSTEN IRVING AND JON STONE

SIDEKICK BOOKS

www.drfulminare.com

First published in 2011 by

Sidekick Books
Flat 38, 23 Mile End Road
London E1 4TN

Printed by
Lavenham Press Ltd
47 Water Street
Lavenham CO10 9RN

Typeset in Sylfaen
Birdbook title font: DaDa Antiquerist
Dr F's signature font: Wet Dream
Sidekick Books logo font: Roman Antique

~

Acknowledgements:
'Goldfinches' by Judith Lal first appeared in *Flageolets at the Bazaar*
(Smith/Doorstop, 2006)

ISBN: 978-0-9564164-3-8

Contents

Broad-leaved Woodland

Coniferous Woodland

Introduction

EVERY bird in the British Isles, documented in one book, in verse and illustration, utilising the latest generation of word-agitators and pen-wrigglers. This was my original vision. An extensive trawl through my archives uncovered a single 1969 edition of The Reader's Digest Book of British Birds, which listed, to my surprise, over 200 such species. Who knows how many more have sprung from the nooks of creation in the intervening years? Thus I was convinced by my under-editors to limit myself to the birds listed in the aforementioned book, and to spread the project across four volumes, split by habitat. This is but the first volume, with others to follow if it is moderately successful.

One could speculate endlessly on the continuing appeal of these small and multifarious creatures. It might be that, hemmed in as we increasingly are by technology, urban development and each other, they persist in reminding us of our neglected natural environment. It might be that in their wide spectrum of appearances and behaviours they shine a vital, unflattering light on the uniformity of our practices. Or it might be a kind of Darwinian appeal – that an abundance of flighty fellows is a sign of the kind of healthy, nurturing landscape where our shovel-jawed ancestors could safely settle.

Such speculation is really for another time and another book. In this one, that fascination, whatever its explanation, is merely the starting point. It remains only for me to extend a few token slivers of my personal gratitude to that raft of poets and illustrators who have answered the call to arms with such fat-hearted enthusiasm, and to you, petulant reader, for investing in this volume. Adequately done!

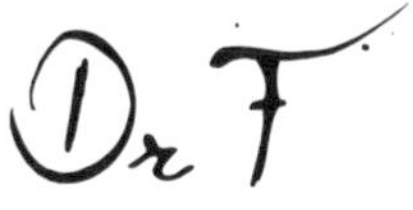

DR FULMINARE
(Editor-in-chief, Sidekick Books)

TOWNS

Black-headed gull

Black-headed gull

Larus ridibundus

Isobel Dixon

The Parliament of Gulls

Fresh on the shingle,
the upturned seagull-
gutted baby sharks,
eye sockets scooped-out
holes in sheeted flesh,
a spectral gathering
of Ku Klux fish.
Sated, a sarky
seagull parliament's
in session on the beach:
the speaker struts
and scoffs, a preachy
scavenger. Nearby
we plunder pebbles
from the rattling strand,
our pockets filled
with mottled planets
and a cock-eyed earth
cupped in my open hand.

Starling

Starling

Sturnus vulgaris

Holly Hopkins
Starlings

I'd heard the fens were dying seas
pinned into their beds by reeds;
the sedges crowded out our path
through the washed-out winter marsh.

They came in ragged lines that fell
into the budding, chirping swell
of bodies caught up in a flow
that stretched itself like kneaded dough

until the churning shoal was black
and hemmed within a living sack
that smashed itself across the dusk
but could not break the thread of trust

that held each bird beside another
and pulled the molten flock together
until they turned and, plunging down,
were hooked into the weedy ground.

We both stood locked inside our coats
and in the dark we neither spoke
in case our clumsy blundering
upset the other's newfound wings.

Black redstart

Black redstart

Phoenicurus ochruros

Rachael Allen
Rag Bird

'During and after the Second World War the population boomed as a consequence of the Blitz. The bombsites of the City provided an ideal habitat.'

The birds became the seams, but looked un-seamed
like the thousands of rags created through war. De-peopled, unspined

the ghost clothes flew in to bank on the man-made screes
beneath the V A S E L I N E advert, stuck on in a spirit white.

A spirit, white like the ones vicars thought passed up through churches.
Vicars who would hope, when reburying the already-dead, blown feet away

from their graveyards, that these far-flung spirits would be able to find
their way back up through the damage

to where the birds watched everything. From their populous high place,
their aphrodisiac scree, they clothed the city with their non-stop breeding.

I heard for every building that lost a body, two birds moved in,
and some people said it looked like they were laughing.

House sparrow

Passer domesticus

House sparrow

Dave Coates

House Sparrow

My sparrow is dying. But that can wait. The Romans
named her *passer*, taking in the sense of speed
that bloomed to what is fleeting, or passion,
that sense of headlong flightpaths that push her splayed

wingtips to the edges of control. The whole
intricate piping of her body anchors
itself to life in increments, doses of will,
her fugitive play. When you say that the blur

between daylight and the dark seems no broader
than this fault-lined pill that animates your vitals,
you're not a million miles from the truth, my sparrow,

but let the waiting be long. May your last recital
embody this growing proximity to tomorrow,
may you lose your voice in song at this darkening border.

Swift

Swift

Apus apus

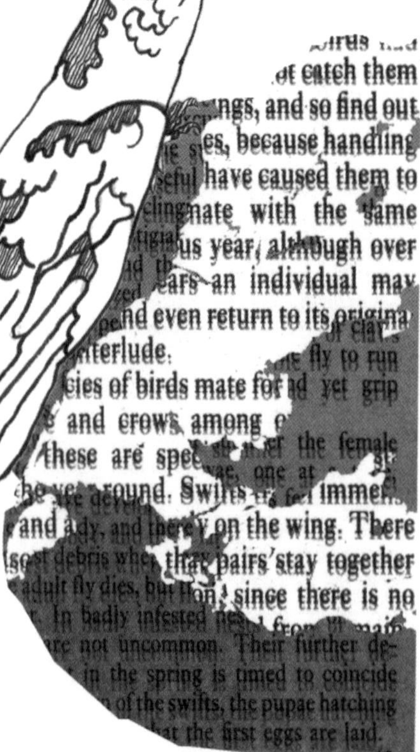

JON STONE

I'm Naming The Swifts

Soots Schrei

Hardtooth Quirk

Quickstitch Chicane

Flechette

Scissorz Hairpin

Pinwheel

Soon-to-be

Starproof Ushkuinik

Hatpin

Sure-to-be

Haraka

Dao

Pinjig

Guadana

Jinks

Nofoot

Weatherknot

Ninepin

Tanto

Pinstripe

Bat O'Noon

Ohanzee

Skyfish

Burningken

House martin

Delichon urbica

House martin

Richard Price
House Martins

Back at the old place, I saw two house martins
high up the gable wall.
None had sought to nest there before,
to spit their muddy puddles out and form a property.
They'd preferred our neighbours' period roof:
the protection, the liberty of ample decoration.
The darkness there was always more generous,
a home-maker's salvation – pretty, but hurricane-proof.

Now one further martin flitted in.
As darkness thickened, dusk's exhilaration thinned.
The three gripped the roughcast:
steep to good sense they settled to survey, confer, to attest
(they're squat little scraps at rest). From a blue-black sketch-of-a-guess
they solidified to a delegation, a thorough inspectorate of doubt.

I called softly, then softly. Less softly again (not quite a shout). At last
my daughtered clattered out in pink, trademarked clobber.
She stopped, though, at my conspirator's look – she saw,
stepped carefully closer. Together we restored
the hush beneath our tired travellers.

A little later she fetched her phone, but didn't chatter.
Instead she captured digitally those soft, angular shapes,
if just as specks (she had no flash, no zoom).

The eaves were empty when I visited next,
early evening / late afternoon.
The martins must have weighed that scant shelter's future –
measured tomorrow, or made the attempt; debated at length.
They'd paused; paused. Decided against.

Feral pigeon

Feral pigeon

Columba livia

Cliff Hammett
Looms over Looms

I can't recall seeing a pigeon
on a telephone line, perhaps you only see
the lines in the country, I can't remember
the last pigeon I threw bits
of bread to,
or the last time I felt
the rattling of the railway bridge,
though it's just over the way, maybe
I'm asleep when the freight
trains pass;
once I arrived, feared
the keys were gone, slipped out a pocket
hole and clattered on the wet pavement
just as coins do, stitching's not
what it was,
trousers last
hardly a month before I needle them,
since quitting post had been out of work
for a year, out of the habit of replacing
things,
but the keys
were there all right, dug into a gap
in the seam, clawed in like a chick unready
to be shoved out the nest
just yet;
and I can still hear
my old flatmate yelling "flying rats"
as he threw the pigeon's eggs at their heads,
they'd taken over the balcony and at last
he'd cracked,
whereas I'd enough
of him, so before the lease was up,
left him a letter and moved back
in with my folks for as long
as they'd bear me,

wasn't long
as it happens, so there I was.
Tugged out the key, a fair few
threads with it, stuck it
into the padlock
and swung open
the factory door – to a sound from the rafters,
echoing down crust-speckled walls to the puddles
gathering between rusted machines,
the sound of
the little bastards cooing.

PARKS and GARDENS

Tawny owl

Strix aluco

Tawny owl

ROWYDA AMIN

Night Work

From your bed, noctilucent paths
are rambling, one of which could lead
through the Tudor knot of yew hedge
to that rose arbour at its centre
where white-slippered sleep is breathing.

Simple to untangle one path after the next
if you still had all night, but fat mice
are eating through the blue and green wool
with which the maze is tapestried.

Though tawny owls, silver-beaked, dive
to unpick the plump bodies, bursting
every pink and yellow cross-stitch,
you're still awake at dawn, tattered
in your threadbare nest of bones.

Collared dove

Collared dove

Streptopelia decaocto

Matt Merritt

I.D.

The Germans have you so much better.
Die Fernsehtaube, the television dove.
And yes, each time my screen
shudders and slurs to a double image

I know you're up there, as much
a part of the furniture of suburbia
as the aerial itself, and less than
a lifetime ago, every bit

as exotic, as hypothetical.
I know you're up there,
a double image yourself, usually,
that doubles and doubles again

wherever, whenever we turn our backs,
reciting your emphatic amphibrachs
to move our urban pastoral away
from the chiffchaff and the great tit

and their tired old iambics.
I know you're up there –
ubiquitous ornament, ruthless colonist,
bucker of trends, ersatz cuckoo.

I know you're up there, halfway through
the lazy circles of your display, hanging in the air
like the question you keep asking yourself.
Who are you? Who ARE you?

Song thrush

Song thrush

Turdus philomelos

Roddy Lumsden

Ten Things You Ought to Know About the Song Thrush

one A thrush begins where a struggle has ended
and sweetness rises in new grass.

two The thrush is not a please and thank you bird
and does not resort to laughter.

three The thrush sits nimbly between thrum and thrust –
two words he knows no need for.

four The egg of the thrush is the blue of the water
in the Well of the World's End.

five When the song thrush meets a violet with one eye,
he meets his most equal.

six In winter, spark a candle at your smallest window
and a thrush will tarry nearby with his song.

seven The thinker exalts the thrush, for he runs from
metaphor to metaphor, misease in a coat of allure.

eight If all the thrushes of the thicket vapourised,
then the world would drift in space.

nine Once dead, a song thrush can be rolled thin
and used as a map of any downlands.

ten To remember a thrush, give him a regal name
and pin him to your memory.

Mistle thrush
Turdus viscivorus

Mistle thrush

DECLAN RYAN

Mistle Thrush

The trees were bare, stripped, in this strange land.
        Rain bruised welts onto pale skin. You whimpered,
a struck dog's voice slinking from your mouth.
        Your lips, stained from eating mistletoe berries,

could not pronounce the names for the lost leaves
        or recall the words of cradle songs. A storm-cock cried,
his accent clipped. What his machine-gun evensong
        told of the snapped branches, I was unaware.

Blackbird

Blackbird

Turdus merula

Amy Key

Poem to a Year Lived In Camberwell Road

Times I felt caught under a cut-glass tumbler
– the light high and brittle – as when I was a child

and thought myself alone in the polished-wood
church, nervy and rapt. Other times, porous –

in the bathtub soaking up the citrine charge
of streetlamps. At night, my ambition

was road closures and all the nightlight sealed out.
The treacle-glazed floorboards invited contact.

When alone, I'd lie flat, my spine eking
itself flush to the ground. Often I was not alone,

but mainly I wiped down surfaces,
fetched the wine with ardent domesticity.

In the garden, blackbirds reliably tugged up
the worms; I burned the leaves.

Memories of that year's flowers gather:
celebration roses, daffodils almost gone sour,

an upset of lilies, delivered boxed-up like a Hoover.
Some I preserved, pressed like flesh in a surge.

Ornaments crowded the available surfaces.
Weekly, I added to their number,

as though I could borrow their delicacies,
dissolve the most drear of days.

Robin

Robin

Erithacus rubecula

BETHANY SETTLE
Robin

The dark day I first
Grasped intuition
Robin
You were my reward
Lesson:
That which is needed
May be singing
To you
From several miles away
I learnt backwards,
Years later,
Now

Dipdipping
Chitchitchitting
You sung me
What is
Beneath skin, feathers
Atoms
So light – reboned, rescaled
I watched me from you
How hungry we both were

Now, years later,
We sing in all directions
We are the same,
Robin. Light,
Matter has dressed you in red,
But I can put it on
(And most days, do)

Dunnock

Dunnock or hedge sparrow
Prunella modularis

Aiko Harman
Hedge Sparrows

Perched on the edge of an old wood stool,
he tips back the brim of his flat cap to dab the dew –
You would have loved this, he says to the silence.
He surveys their garden: the honeysuckle buds
sunbathing, the first raspberries bursting burgundy
from green. He looks to the wrought iron chair
where she used to sit, barking gardening tips:
Don't forget to fill the feeders! Leave some seeds
on the ground for the shy ones! My lovelies!

Dull sleek faux sparrows, dunnocks seem nervous
and agitated, constantly flicking their wings and tail.

He remembers the first birds, too timid to take
from the feeders she had always kept brimming.
And watching her prune the hedge, leaving bits of moss
and twigs for nesting, citing some secret discovery.
Now they come each day, expecting what he too longs
to expect: her shock of white hair, the wrought iron
chair filled with instructions. And like the birds,
he returns only to silence.

Their song is a pleasant surprise: a slow sweet
warble or a short, fast, squeaky 'tseep tseep'.

A small brown-grey bird, quiet and shy, creeps
along the edge of the flowerbed on its own, shuffling,
flicking its wings as it goes. He watches the bird
court the scattered seeds; a new bird lands beside her.

The dunnock does not breed in pairs, but groups.
Polyandrous, polygynous, few are monogamous.

She turns her back to her suitor, tail flitting feverish
in the air on display. The suitor dashes fast against her:
first mating. She darts just as fast into the blooming
ceanothus. Another suitor waits below the bush's spray.

His chest puffed, fluffed up, he croons to her. She flirts,
flickers her tail as before. And now the old man spies
this new spry suitor dash against her. Twice mated.
What cheek! he says aloud again, looks to the chair.

Females often court new males whilst already
mated. Both males will feed the brood,
neither sure who the true father is.

The chair is empty still and how could she have loved
these strange beasts, he is thinking, frantic to tell
the silence what he has seen. She will have seen it too,
he thinks, sent them maybe to shake him up.
That's her way. He turns to see the fair grey down
of his neighbour's crown slip from the tip of their
shared fence just quick enough to surprise him.

Wren

Troglodytes troglodytes

Wren

Matthew Gregory

The Wren

Through one long passage there is another
and through another
the dining hall
of the Hôtel Saint-Pol, and there, the King.
He's at supper, over his latest caprice –
the wren.
He picks at it with his oyster fork
and opens the chest
with the sharp side, turning out the meat
from the hairbone gristle
and the locked breast.
He unlocks the bird.
The flesh is silver and pink and even remarkable.
The breast opens
like the two halves of a peach.
Zut alors. This is the King speaking.
Zut alors.
Instead of the tiny heart, lungs, liver,
the organ's wet beads,
there is another, smaller bird inside the first.
And, another.
Three, four, five bloodied miniatures
cased inside the one before.
With his bright little *canif*
the King slices into a sixth successive wren
not much bigger than a thimble.

He might expect to find something writ
on the innards of that last bird,
a key, in its filigree of guts.
But still the King sits up,
extracting wren from wren
until there are no wrens
anywhere, at all, in the Hôtel Saint-Pol.

Great tit

Great tit

Parus major

Emily Hasler

Great Tit

that see me seeme seeme
makes me want to see

the bird that makes the news
sings louder in cities

flaunts its plumage
has been known to murder bats

flirtatious, unfaithful
divorce is common

and a means to survival
see me seeme seeme

the colourful titmouse
says the medieval bestiary

is a bird curious about other birds

whether dead or alive
they'll come to look

not because they care
because they are curious

they think the world is a mirror or a book

and thus we may catch them
while they search for their selves

Blue tit

Blue tit

Parus caeruleus

CAROLINE CREW

Acrobatic

"Observe the greatness of China," demands the ringmaster's
disembodied voice. His arms spread and in their upward arc
the acrobats are embraced: lithe bodies crumple on red silk,
curl to cannonballs and firework in any inhuman direction.
I think that China must be a land of swoops and everything
in balance, like the bird table outside: the expert blue tits
poise on twig points, tightrope along the washing line
and toss peanuts like those painted girls from the trapeze.
How dangerous China's greatness must be, the precise
orchestration of its whipped swirls with no safety net,
how unlike the blue tits perfectly ensconced in air.

Greenfinch

Greenfinch
Carduelis chloris

JUDITH LAL

Greenfinch

Dapper in olive
Spruced as wild canary
Of back of beyond
Dipping and waving
Bodyboarding suburbs
Wearing socking reflectors
Sunstroked dandy
With basted pockets
Plying sunflowers
Bright hearted
Frowning star
Scorched beautiful
On the longest day
Busy in that beauty
Talk of the town
Dzweee dzweee
With husky mouthpiece
Falling out with your song
Dropping an unclosed field
Into the conversation
Then flowers where
You left an accident
Of table manners
And the lawn reverts
From a green spittoon

Chaffinch

Chaffinch

Fringilla coelebs

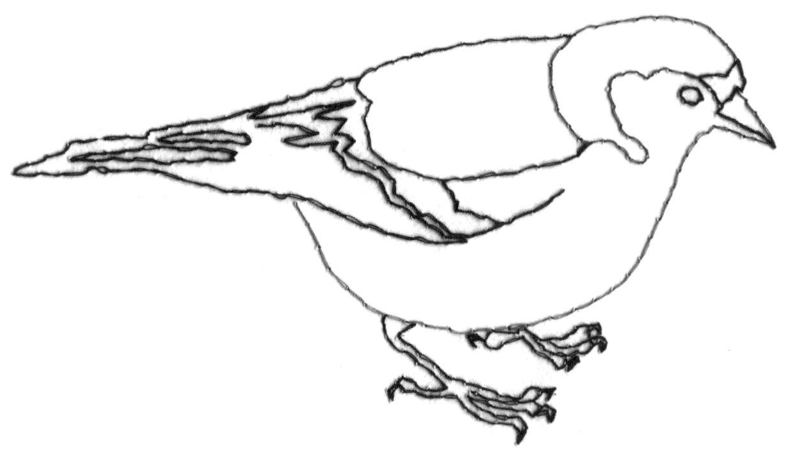

EMILY HASLER

St Jerome and the Chaffinch

More usually with a lion he can't shake off,
and always with a book – but,
sometimes, he appears with a chaffinch.

Animals love him. And it's a symbol
of celibacy to be accompanied by a chaffinch.
The colourful male winters less far away than his mate.

He becomes known as the bachelor bird
and also the harbinger of rain.
But only sometimes does he sing for rain,

other times he sings for sun, or for his mate.
The French say *gay comme un pinson*
but we are not always so gay

or so serious. Bosch paints him this way.
I cannot say why he sings, only that
the chaffinch, sometimes, appears with St Jerome.

Bullfinch
Pyrrhula pyrrhula

MATT MERRITT

Bullfinch

Caged fool,
   thrall to the bird flute's two thin notes.
Industrious glutton,
   the nurseryman's bounty red upon your neck.
A finished masterpiece,
   shadowed by its own preliminary sketch.
An embarrassed tuning-up,
   that couldn't carry this far, could it?
From here, a muddy golf ball
   bouncing away out of bounds.
A brief blazon,
   only really known once gone.

Goldfinch

Carduelis carduelis

JUDITH LAL
Goldfinches

A charm of goldfinches visit when I'm not home.
They pull cobwebs from my door saying,

we who represent the infinite riches of heaven,
called by today and found you not in,
it is a pity we missed you.

I imagine they sound like Kathmandu.

Spotted flycatcher

Spotted flycatcher

Muscicapa striata

Simon Barraclough

Spotted Flycatcher

Your metaphors have got me real down,
man,
have grounded my fleet.
My members refuse
to scissor shapes of sky
or quilt the o'erclouding blue
with busy stitching beaks
and when we speak
(and we don't really speak)
it's not Morse Code, you know.
I'm a taut sac of giblets,
an urge to shit and screw,
I do not soar, I flee,
and man, I hate this food.

Waxwing

Waxwing

Bombycilla garrulus

Edward Mackay

Waxwing

I had sewn myself into a sailcloth shroud
of blue, stitched around me with the needle
of my sing-song laughter: my earth-bound

epitaph written on the evening. And I fell.
A burning blistered down my hands, slipped
out the stream, unsealed from air, torn down

in the tumbling turn. My father thrust
my salt-licked tangle of feather, limb and dust
into the jealous blackness of earth.

But that soaring thrill's not shaken from
my shattered bones – the swallowed sky clings
to the cloud of my fallen heart, flickering

in my throat, breathing me awake tonight.
Seized by height, scared of sun, a crumpled leg
jerks up. Arms shake to ragged wings: I clamber

out of boyish flesh, feel Grecian sun still throbbing
in the earth. I take fright, tumble into reclaimed flight
that smoothes my matted blood-stuck hair

into a feathered peak, panicked eyes turn
outwards. Sunrise cracks the edge of night
and turns the fist of me towards the cold.

That blue above, that bright blue, under me,
shining off the cooling snow. The higher sun,
undone from danger. The badge of all I've been

clings like a past to my wingtips. I set my beak
like a compass needle, north. I sing the chill into the sky
and wear my wax to spite the claim of surface things.

Hoopoe

Hoopoe

Upupa epops

Isobel Dixon
Upupa Epops

Scarce passage migrant regular enough to skim the south
of this glib outcrop with your pied and pinkish now-and-then
but still, erratic flitter on the wing, old vaudevillean,
knowing that you'll cause a flutter on the wires.

A prophet less respected in those backyard days
you poked about our frazzled lawn, a dandy priest.
Familiarity and all the blah it breeds.
Who knew, so dapper in your black-barred

cinnamon-cum-chestnut raiment, you'd turn out to be,
back home, a smelly nester of the first degree?
The sins fine feathers and a rather natty crest can hide.
Oop-oop-oops, indeed.

Your Giant St Helena Ancestor went dodo,
long before Napoleon and the Giant Earwig did.
But still you pop up here and there, to stride and plunge
that beaky scythe, delving the underworld for breakfast –

spiders easy over, ant lions sunny side up,
a take-out gogga, kriek or two to feed the brood.
You foul your hidden clutch of milky-blue. Tree-caved,
surviving critters shit at probing eyes, and hiss like snakes.

Broad-leaved WOODLAND

Woodcock

Woodcock

Scoppolax rusticola

Matt Merritt

Watching Woodcocks, 25.4.10

The birdwatcher's problem becomes the poet's.

How to remain within the frame, yet unobserved.
How to frame something that is in a moment
more bat than bird,
more branch than bat,
more leaf-mould than branch.

How to sift countless stories.
A bird witlesse enough to be trodden on
yet capable of carrying its young
away from danger on its back. A bird
that escapes the dog days
by flying to the moon.

How to use that prized pin-feather.
For fishing-flies. For fans. For removing
motes from eyes. In ancient China,
for stimulating the clitoris.
For painting woodcock
flickering at the edge of vision.

How to make yourself
more camera than birdwatcher or poet
before you are gone
into the black bead of its eye.

Sparrowhawk

Sparrowhawk
Accipiter nisus

JUDITH LAL

Sparrowhawk Mews

I have none of the hundred, thousands, millions of sparrows
that we sung of in school,
how God knew every one of them as God knew me,
yet you come with no hood or bells

from not far off god yourself,
for a holy stuffed brace
of snow-shaken, brainfrozen blackbird,
medieval spread of bird dolled inside bird.

It is a cleanly quick operation
of red on white suburbs
with the glance of small volcanoes
burning up through Habitat Deco.

The crackle of neurons through the night have reached the end of
a sharp branch.

This moment like a feather in an ice cube.

You enter the nipped morning fresh from a dry bath,
silently brushed over with a white broom,
towelled off with wind chill,
preened with the beak of a new year in your chest,
cold against a breath,

combing through inclement scrub.

The hollowness trapped between things keeps you warm,
wood spirals and flyleaf pages of snow,
in fiercely guarded solitude of winter's allowance,
fit for a priest and below a Marlyon for a lady.

The space your eyes take up
is more than an estate's worth.
The world has eyes for you
and yours are made in the great factory of eyes.

Through them the short day is magnified up to its eyeballs.
So I won't call you canary in this coalmine,
just unblinking bettered smartness
where I am still a guest
diluted at kitchen window.

You leave for nowhere I know, perfectly balanced
    with two suns in winter.

Red kite
Milvus milvus

Nia Davies

Kite

Scavenger of contours,
circling the meat road,
the cars have thrown up your lunch.

We roll back the roof,
swerving, slowing,
to watch your red-wedge flukes,

as you retake the beacons,
reclaiming your mewing parks,
your Strata Florida.

This is our second chance to love you,
pest and puttock,
to show you we care for you,

grave-tearer,
claws begotten of blackthorn,
flytip clearer, iron-age dart.

We pull over while you doodlebug down
for your fast food rabbit.
There is no fear of metal.

Roadkill could make you roadkill,
but you take everything back,
in the green hilt of hills.

Buzzard

Buzzard

Buteo buteo

AIKO HARMAN

The Rollercoaster

As we drove through a hilly, wooded part
of south Devon a couple weeks ago
you spotted some early purple orchids
on a grass verge next to the road.

I pulled into a lay-by. You jumped out
to check the flowers, and with the engine off
I could hear a buzzard's plaintive Peee-uu,
                                        Peee-uu

They haunt the woods here now, sit hours
motionless on the boughs of trees, watching
patiently for some small rabbit, bird or reptile
to pass.
                                        I looked up –
a lone adult circled high above me,
her broad wings taut to their full five feet.
Seconds later, I clocked another
speeding towards her.

The calls intensified. I had a feeling
something fierce was in the offing.
To think, these flockless beasts that feed
on carrion – scraps left to rot, forgotten trash –
could be so particular about their partners:
                                        pairs mate for life.

The incoming bird swooped low, peaked:
reached the first bird and both whirled
around on each other, face to face for an instant,
talons touching as they fell through the air
in barrel rolls, a roller coaster, a gyre spiral –
the coming of a new era – and then split,
flew off in opposite directions.

You'd plucked the orchids. We returned to the car,
the road. You asked if I'd seen them 'dancing':

fields full of buzzards stomping the fresh earth
their feet like a rainstorm, luring worms to surface.
They'd smell to heaven.
                                        You sketched the orchids
in your lap, pulp dripping on the floor-mat.
I thought of the roller coaster,
if I had ever risked myself to impress you.
If I could stay with you forever after just one dance.

Wryneck

Wryneck

Jynx torquilla

KIRSTEN IRVING
Wryneck

The little archaeologist steps carefully, long-nosedly
examining the trench. His documentary is an ongoing special
on the history of his own. Every so often a find

will flash beneath his quad-pronged claw, and he'll dip, then turn
excitedly to camera, describing the dark pod of the British scarab,
and its role as a delicacy (to illustrate, he pops the trinket,

wriggling, into his craw – *actually* delicious!) at the height
of the Jynx dynasty. Scratching further, he'll tell you
of the mysteries that many believe contributed

to the eventual fall of the empire, and the exile into poverty
of the nobles (many of whom, he points out, would have shed
their mail and silks for a colour not entirely dissimilar

to that of my own mud-spackled coat. A symbol of the earth
and its fruits, or simply camouflage? We may never know).
In the next programme, he will investigate whether the Jynx

were, as is claimed, a fictional clan, or whether, in some hut
leaning on the sea, the last descendant is making cloaked love
to a peasant's son, the two of them knotted like woodgrain.

Great spotted woodpecker

Great spotted woodpecker

Dendrocopos major

JAMES WILKES

Great Spotted Woodpecker

Heath liquefied, acid earth rind as a sea might be: painted rolling flecked with titanium white or the grand simplicity of a change of state, in a lunar eclipse perhaps or noon when ghosts appear. Floating over this the power lines of the contemporary past, corralling pine wood into geopolitics; we hate being netted in the old shapes of constant vigilance, which had us thrashing sullenly through dust and sunlight. Perspectives open then snap shut. Across this, the looping movement of a large bird, a deep thunderclap as two jets buzz the woodpecker.

Lesser spotted woodpecker

Dendrocopos minor

Lesser spotted woodpecker

James Wilkes
Lesser Spotted Woodpecker

We would like to know when all these deer actually *work* as you never see them at it. Their spoor is stacked in the form of logs. A plastic chair nailed halfway up a tree. Climbing into its cup we surmise it is for shooting the deer if they fail to complete their quotas. A death perspective snaps open. Across this, the looping movement of a slight bird. It all goes strangely quiet as it drums a hollow tattoo of ants and bracken in the smell of rain-to-come.

Green woodpecker

Green woodpecker

Picus viridis

James Wilkes

Green Woodpecker

A parabolic storm mirror ploughed with phosphates. Stage for an operetta known as A History of Commoning Paid Off; Or, The Where and How of Exploitation Change. Act 1 is afforestation with occasional outbreaks of zeal, Act 2 is thinning with frequent policy later. The mirth flows readily throughout. Across this, the looping movement of a green bird. Laughter and snapping in the forest as rain clouds unroll down the channel.

Turtle dove

Streptopelia turtur

Turtle dove

ROWYDA AMIN

Zugunruhe

Yes, you've been the freckled darling
of all the rooftop cabarets,

your high kicks petalling the town
with cheap scanties – but now you're the one

left singing after the music has ended
so it's time to get the suitcase down,

pack those veneerial fripperies,
make a plan to fly south.

Nightingale

Nightingale

Luscinia megarynchos

Amy Key

I Haven't Had A Dream For A Long Time

Again I'm awake in a room full of dark, like cola
gone flat, thinking of those bodies, parallel to mine,

lying in their own attic rooms; and the plump pigeons
roosting. To have always wanted an attic.

Today, the pavement webbed my sandals to the ground
with a feeling like candyfloss stuck to fingers.

Then there was the dirt, huddled in each fold
of my feet. I bathed them in the salad bowl, before bed,

and sliced cucumber for my eyes.
I don't understand it's too hot to eat.

The sound of police at this hour makes me say
'constabulary' out loud to disprove my suspicion

I may have forgotten how. Tomorrow, for tea,
something gagged with salt; freshly picked peas.

A nightingale sings. It seems I do sleep.

Redstart

Phoenicurus phoenicurus

Redstart

Chrissy Williams
Redstart

I wanted to find a crying redstart even though Grandad said they don't exist any more but people are always telling me things don't exist any more and the land used to go much higher than this with flowers like lemongrass lovehearts and such growing up right out of the ground but whatever I don't care I happen to like the sighing heat that runs this lava weir under our feet and anyway doesn't life always find a way I thought that's what the narrator said.

The redstart sounds
its hurried cry.
I buy a postcard.

Pied
flycatcher

Pied flycatcher
Ficedula hypoleuca

Simon Barraclough

Pied Flycatcher

You and I know the meaning of 'pied',
we're educated types,
subscribe to BBC Wildlife.
But charnel skies
are crammed with cannibals, kestrels, kites
that spy with their side-mounted eyes
wingèd canapés, savoury bites,
wee beaky vol-au-vents in flaky flight.

Fortunately, falcons make poor pastry chefs,
their greedy grapnels good and gunged
like pigeon feet on London streets
that sink into moist chewing gum,
which hardens into stiff concrete
to leave them hobbled, knobbled,
pinching off their blood supply
until the gummy hybrid claw's scraped off
by trudging round Trafalgar Square.
Now, where was I?

Blackcap
Sylvia atricapilla

Edward Mackay
Tacc Tacc, Blackcap

Tacc tacc;   creetily creetily – akerah creektur
turrturr   *You will be taken hence* turr creetily creetily:
akerah, *and from there*   creetur creetur –
turrturr,   *to a place*   akerah akerah creetah.
a place Akertah! *of lawful*   tacc tacc
creetur *execution*   tacc tacc…   creetilly tacc
where you will be creetily creetily tac tac
hanged tacc tacc *by the neck* creetily
until dead tacc tacc. *And may the* creetily akerah tac
Lord tacc tacc *have mercy* creetily *on your*
tacc tacc akerah *soul.*   Tacc.

Garden warbler

Garden warbler

Sylvia borin

Niall Campbell
Garden Warbler

Were you to call the name we've given you,
you too would call out *Garden Warbler.* Garden Warbler
instead of your own song. That click and whistle.

That click and whistle song encompassing yourself,
your mate and brood in the warm nest; your shared,
brown cloak, brown beak, and lighter underbelly;

the fields of grass, too, and their stricken leaves;
the river; the moss rock you've stopped on;
the orb of light, and its paler twin come dark;

and somewhere in this, names for us who watch you.
You've just the one song, sometimes shorter, sometimes
longer, for this: the whole meadow, the May-fly.

Chiffchaff

Phyllloscopus collybita

Tom Chivers

Chiffchaff

two notes   the remote unlocking of a car   chiffchaff
chiffchaff   squeak of rubber sole   on linoleum   your

ballooning concave of breast   discoloured vellum   may hide the
engorged larva of a tick   feeding on your   blood   chiffchaff

paranoid jerks   scope   the field   Nikon   chiffchaff   chiffchaff
as the day turns to soupy blue   what ghostly figures

do you see   chiffchaff   at the hedgeline blotchy   grieving

cling as bull   whose pockets sing   chiffchaff
with silver   tithes   and tribulations

Willow warbler

Willow warbler

Phylloscopus trochilus

SIOFRA MCSHERRY

Willow Warbler

A night migrant, the willow warbler
is believed to navigate by the stars,
although this cannot be proved.
Winter weathering in West Africa,
twice a year he quarters the globe
with the handspan of himself,
to wash his wings in the hot sand,
chasing summer, chasing light.

He leaves us with winter,
which is just as true as summer
but empty of warblers.
We are left with the cold truth of it,
the freezing, the shutting down,
the narrowing, and the wait.

Wood warbler

Phyllosoopus sybilatrix

Wood warbler

Nia Davies

Wood Warbler

In the unaxed oak
and the underleaf,
where a feast hatches
for a hidden eater or
a smallish singer,
a Thai green belly
is patched over by tree.

And it blows those calls:
a reedy woodwind
with kora playing
tapped melodics,

trying to elbow in
a slice of bandwidth
amongst Buzzard,
Thrush and Chiffchaff,

hipping up the trunk
with a draw-string beak,
shutting-up from singing
till there's hush
in the barging forest,

till there's space in
the rustling arena,
from the chainsaw
and the twitcher,
and all those other
tiny gladiators
tangling for flies.

Long-tailed tit

Long-tailed tit

Aegithalos caudatus

Lizzy Dening
Dot Dash Dot

This patterned ribbon

binds the saplings

cross-stitching

sky and land.

Dipping

his sheath
of tail

frantically
like a coded message.

Each head

bob telling me something

engrained in every tree trunk, every

newly opened bud something

about the nature

of survival. About more haste more speed,

about the
one hundred thousand ways
there are to

make an exit.

Marsh tit

Marsh tit

Parus palustris

Andrew Jamison

Marsh Tit Poem

I've had to take this brand new page for a marsh tit
for even a bird with a name like 'marsh tit' needs space
to ruffle, shake out, marsh tit itself into.

Ruffle, shake out, marsh tit, between these Moleskine margins.

Beyond all margins, and space itself, there is a marsh tit
silenced by a sense of its own marsh tit-ness,
not chirping or singing or twitter-tweeting – marsh titting.

Remember, marsh tit, to stay exactly as you are.
marsh and tit in the ways you have been taught
by all of your fellow marsh titters.
Remember, marsh tit, your mother? Mother marsh tit?

Before all mothers, and birth itself, was a marsh tit.
Marshing and titting was all it did, knew how to do
in the marshy, titbit days we've come to call the beginning.

Marsh tit, remember those days? All there was was you.

After everything, and nothing itself, will come a marsh tit.

Willow tit
Parus montanus

JOHN CLEGG

Willow Tit

Her beak is a split thorn
carving a zipline,
undressing the seedpod.

Ignore her calls,
those sudden shudders
of breath in a pinetree.

Ignore her completely.
Some birds in China
sculpt nests from spit;

she'll hammer a home
in your huge neglect,
eyeshadowed, black-capped.

In the land of the dead
the judges will balance
your heart and her feather.

Treecreeper

Treecreeper

Certhia familiaris

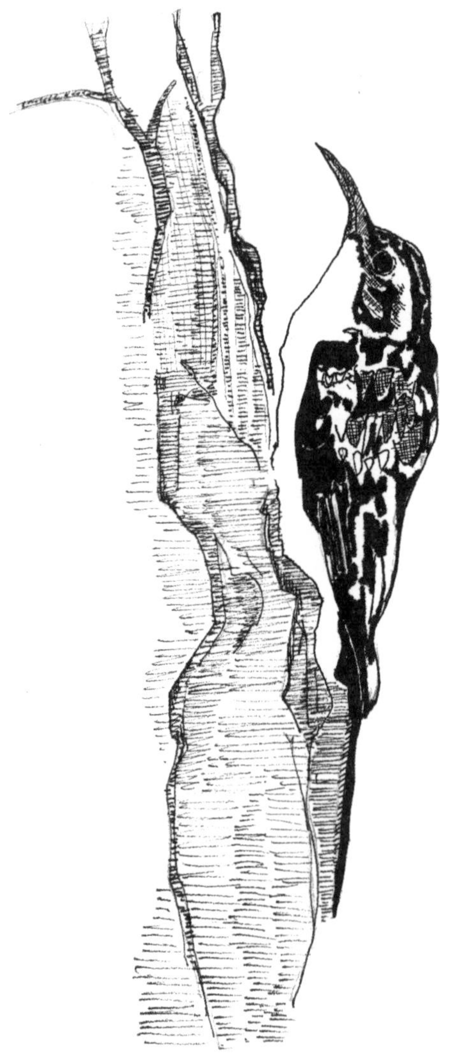

John Clegg
Treecreeper

Bent apple
in the shadow of a cupola,

treecreeper
interrogating the trunk.

Spycatcher.
Pries open a wound in the bark,

dislodges
a spellbound mock-wasp

it bursts
with a jab to the back. Cataloguer

of hidey-holes
feathered with deadwood,

it knows
the caterpillar's schedule

and how to slip
over the border unnoticed

in winter.
It is nobody's national bird.

Nuthatch
Sitta europaea

Kate Potts
Nuthatch

The original name for the nuthatch was 'nut-hack', derived from the bird's habit of fixing nuts in a crevice of the tree's bark and hacking them open with its beak to find the kernel.

The Reader's Digest Field Guide to the Birds of Britain

The story was the thing. I used to keep my subjects
close. I toiled, hacked, and prised –

pure, righteous curiosity, a pick-axe beak, true
and dogged at my driving,

quiet fidgets, wired questioning. Who-when-what-
why-where and how?

Night phonecalls to inside men, clipped meetings
in hunched back rooms, iced whiskies

loosening their weak red tongues. A sly ask in return
for a fingered banknote. All in the right order.

My measure of dug dirt screeched in each story's
tag-line, scandals flagged in scarlet,

in verdana. A scam with the ministry's pension money,
transnational heroin cartels,

a trafficked girl's teeth pulled one by one with pliers
to numb her silent for the border.

Always the cheapest lives expended – for passports,
diamonds, pharmaceuticals, simple

dominance. Nothing new under the sun. Bitter-tired
I'd shuffle, sleepwalk, back to our huddled

rooms and him. Our conversation wheeled and fuddled
back and forth like a spitting sea. We ate

our gritty, home-made loaves, drank good red wine
from camping mugs and sheltered

in each other's wake, against each other's broad
and bullish skin. We saw

our ragged, feckless passing by of years. The world
was various, then.

Brambling

Brambling

Fringilla montifringilla

Holly Hopkins

Brambling

Bird of the beech mast, Cock o' the North,
you gather where trees are greyhounds
and the floor crisp with old pennies.
You hide, spy amongst other flocks,
the hem of your white shirt giving you away.
Brindled bird, you conceal your nest with moss,
soothe the sight of it back into the wood
while you line it with golden hair, fox fur
and down, a plush case for warm stones.

Bird who could lie puddled in my palm
you have been further,
travelled the cold lands, Arctic and Russia,
when they break open rich in summer
with grass and warmth matured under snows,
waiting for when the waters run clear
and mosquitoes catch the long evening light.
Bird with a blushing breast
you flow from there back to us
through arteries which only you can see.

Jay

Garrulus glandarius

JULIA BIRD

Jeff

So, the oaks and the hazels are dripping wet.
That doesn't make this the rainforest.

Parrots, in their car-horn colours
working their fascinator tails

their secateur beaks
and dinned-in roller skating skills,

are not vaulting through the canopy
effing and blinding their pirate eloquence.

We've come here in what will be the last
of your four new red Fiestas.

That flash of brick-dust and bluebell through the leaves,
that one sharp cry – that might have been a jay.

Hawfinch

Hawfinch

Coccothraustes coccothraustes

CAROLINE CREW

Hawfinches

Those cherries weren't cold, not clean even,
but we tongued their flesh greedily.
Dust clung to our juiced faces, the red smear
in your beard bringing out the Viking features.

Their wooden hearts became your weapon,
tongue-propelled and shot with all the speed
your cheeks could muster. I never learnt to spit vicious,
the stones just stumbled off my lips.

It came, the shared vision of seed-spitters, long enough
for trunks to spring up and blossoms unfurl in the mind,
promising an orchard if we ever returned, and fruit.
The corners of our eyes couldn't catch the reapers

waiting in the beeches. Twenty steps down the path
they descended: hawfinches. Bills like scythes,
bodies secretly as dense as lead and determined
to crack each stone with just one blow,

pry apart the damp husks, extract the kernels
like teeth and peck them to mash. They made sure
to destroy anything that might grow: the imagined boughs
trampled by the patter of cherry-stained feet.

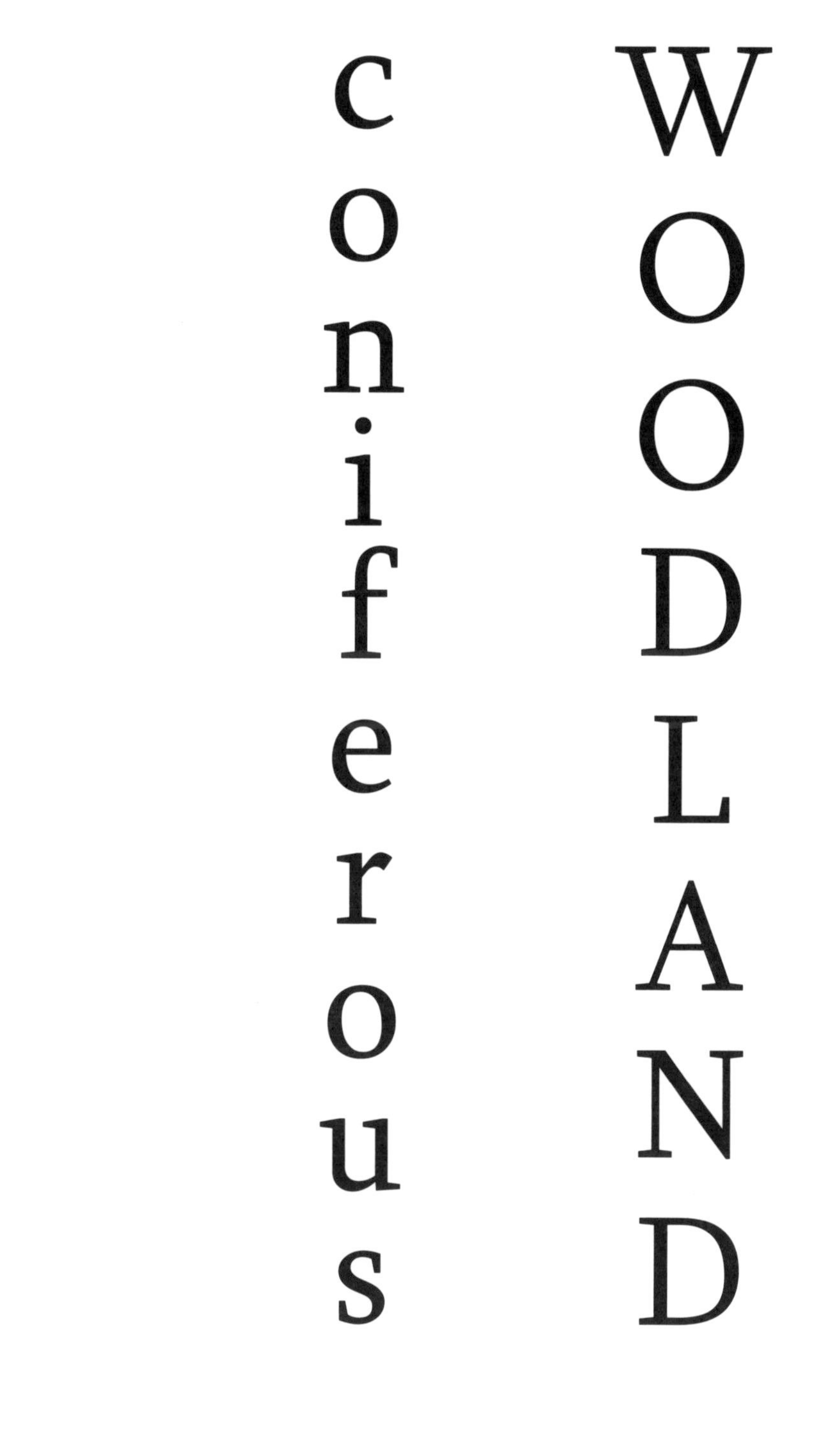
coniferous
WOODLAND

Capercaillie
Capercaillie

Tetrao urogallus

DECLAN RYAN
Capercaillie

Percussion at dawn, eyes rolling to the roses
he spreads out his feathers, this wood-horse,
sky saluter. Lust-drum, sex-cymbal, he taps
out his courting call, blind to the hunter's step,
Sissi – lost in the cross-hairs, his own rhythm.

I too know of rapture, that leafy mire, myth,
sense-depriver, of all the hours I have lost
searching for traces of my rivals in the lattices
of your tights, eager with envy of the elastic
at your wrist, your pulse, deaf to the rifleshots.

Black grouse

Black grouse

Lyrurus tetrix

Dave Coates
Black Grouse

The *whuff* of its wings as it escaped.
The vacuum
of four people's worth of silence. Where does your mind
go in that dip between the waves of something
oncoming and irresistible, as fine and damaging
as the liquor bottles on the shelf that seemed
to root us to the spot, to show up our whatness,
almost crass in our inability to be
anywhere else? Black Grouse, Bombay Sapphire, La Mauny,
the day's entropy emerging the way
                                                                        the bird did
in that blunt surge of memory that rolled over me,
the forked white tail rising like a beacon
as sunlight failed, as it settled somewhere green,
shimmering just beyond my line of sight.
If joy is no
slight thing, neither then is its opposite – not grief,
dynamic and natural as birdsong, but
inertia – not the *whuff* of its wings as it escaped
but the seconds before I could run after it.

Long-eared owl

Long-eared owl

Asio otus

MATT MERRITT

Evidence

Each winter, they shrink to a rumour.
For years, only a low moan
that might have been wind blowing
across the chimney pots,
or a creak and whine
that could have been the rusting gate,
swinging wide just this side of sleep.

But once, half a mile from home
and surprised by the silent swoop
of night, we flushed a flurry
of autumn colour in the lane
and were almost brushed by a breath
of wings, that hardened and darkened
amid the hawthorn thicket, became
a branch tipped by embers

burning up the light's last slivers.
Freed from earth's embrace, with every star
a crucible to kindle from,
so might our eyes fire.
So might we flame on.

Crossbill
Loxia curvirostra

MARION MCCREADY

We Meet by a Charm of Crossbills

The blood-birds kiss the air
as they fall from cone to cone,

their warp of mandibles
freeing the fruits, shucking the shells.

Below them, the sky is flecked
with drifting scales.

You whisper 'crossbills'
and a bird rises in my throat.

You taste of rust and nails.
The Douglas-firs hold up the fiery bells,

their thick bull-necks, their forked tails.
My skin is a spectrogram of your breath.

You spell words with symbols on my neck,
the blood-bird song a warning in our heads.

Scottish crossbill

Scottish crossbill

Loxia scotica

RODDY LUMSDEN

Daredevil

The Scottish crossbill is the only vertebrate unique to the British Isles and was confirmed as a species in 2006 on the basis of having a distinctive bird song, a 'Scottish accent'.

Precarious work, keeping watch on three kestrels
as they scud and lift, patrolling from trough-lip
to paddock-post at Honeydale, seeing through
their evening shift. Yet no sleuth could track
the Scottish crossbill, mazing in a sifting flock
of cousins, or snugged in the innards of a larch
or lodgepole, its zincy chirrup proved unique
by sonograms. Who'd be a namer? Who'd paint
endemic on a door, position the decibel meter,
steep their intruments and slides for the sake
of lethal precision, exacting victory? After years
of triumphs, Knievel only achieved real fame
in the wake of a first near-death-crash. I long to be
the captain of the things which have no names.

Lesser redpoll

Lesser redpoll

Acanthis flammea

Chrissy Williams

The Lesser Redpoll

has perchable feet
and a variable sense
of humour. It winks
when you do
and clockwork trills
reveal nothing.
This passerine bird
of the fringillidae
links multiple thoughts
with a single leap
in a metered mess
of pretention, beaking
the best of itself
and singing. Delight
occurs on an infinite scale.
Imagination not included.

Siskin
Carduelis spinus

Nia Davies
Siskin

The Barley Bird could be hung in the parlour,
amongst the pinched petticoat drapery
and the pastel flourishes.

Traded round the continent in a cage,
kept contained for its tight whirring dance,
until someone left the door open,

and it gripped the bars
and felt a bit for the out-there-air,
a bit of the window sill,

the tasselled lamp,
down a bit and up,
over the landscaped humps,

to the topiary and the snapdragon beds,
making pinged flashes in the sycamores,
where flies hung in heat,

into the churned-on,
crunched-on, juiced-up bits
of the red stalk and the loosening open leaves.

Soon this yellowed shifter tapped the conifers
and breathed itself a peep,
in the new ice shushes

by the cracked-open stream.
Made itself a lichen hoarder,
in the stringy winter woods.

Crested tit
Parus cristatus

Dai George

True Eccentrics

As opposed to those who muck about
just outside the bull's-eye.

So none of your neon-smeared
and perfumed chatterers with heads
forever turned to suss their public.

We're talking here of double-twenty freaks.

Garden-shed Edisons buried with their scroll
of blueprints, as though it were a living wife.

King Tubby keeping trim in his lab,
where you check your collie at the door
and everything honks of solder.

Corinthians and vigilantes.

The crested tit, who darts through the pine
on a lunatic prayer, his headdress splayed.

He takes pause in a rotted bole;
halloos forth with tail-feathers
whirring to the Highlands' outer rim.

Coal tit

Coal tit

Parus ater

Niall Campbell

Songs of the Coal Tit

What – the message of its camouflage.
Pebble, and pebble-dash, the grey rocks
by the root of the deflowered hedge.

*

Coal Tit, in song, delivering
from the rock-face its mantra
borrowed from the silversmiths:
be slow, precise and cautious.

*

It sings at dusk, but sings for what,
the passed day or the night to pass,
its face streaked, as it is,
by both the light and the dark.

*

What is this dark knot stationed
on the bare branch? The bird
at its dead perch, or the shadow
of the rose that grew there?

Goldcrest

Goldcrest
Regulus regulus

Lizzy Dening

Goldcrest

For M.C.

We are anxious all the time, you and I.
I flit from cereal bowl to calendar, to cooling
mug of tea. If you could hold a pen
you would make lists, the way that I do –
on envelopes or the backs of my hands.
I wonder if you sometimes wake in the night
to the wind shivering conifer branches,
and the sense that there are things worth worrying about,
things which can't wait for morning.
It's difficult, being so small,
and that's what others don't realise.
When you weigh only 5g, a new anxiety –
finding feeding grounds, vagrant cats,
the maintenance of heat –
can be a heavy load to bear, particularly
as you have no shoulders to speak of.
Only a golden exclamation mark
punctuating the dusky woodland
to say:
"I am here. I will worry for you.
Go back to sleep."

Contributors

Rachael Allen hails from Cornwall. She co-runs the poetry and art collective Clinic and edits the group's anthologies and pamphlets, the next of which, *Clinic 2*, is due to be released in 2011. She writes reviews for *Ambit* magazine, has worked for newspapers in the US and the UK and has had poetry published in *Hum* magazine. Rachael has written plays for the Edinburgh Fringe in 2008 and 2009, and has had short plays commissioned by, and performed at, the Barbican Theatre in Plymouth, as part of their 2007 and 2008 winter festivals.
www.clinicpresents.com

Rowyda Amin was born in Newfoundland, Canada to parents of Saudi Arabian and Irish origin. In 2009, she received the Wasafiri New Writing Prize. Her work has appeared in a range of magazines and the anthologies *Coin Opera* (Sidekick Books, 2009), *Exposure* (Cinnamon Press, 2010) and *Ten* (Bloodaxe Books, 2010).
www.rowyda.com

Hannah Bagshaw was born in Norwich in 1983. She holds a degree in Fine Art from University of the Arts London and recently completed an AHRC-funded MA in Illustration at Camberwell College of Arts. Hannah's work has appeared in the anthology *Stop Sharpening Your Knives* (Eggbox Publishing, 2010) and online art and culture magazine *Platform*, and she has completed a series of illustrations for a modern take on 'The Dance of Death', due to be released this autumn. More recently, she has undertaken illustration work, including logo design, for new magazine *The Brute*.
www.hannahbagshaw.co.uk

Becky Barnicoat draws cartoons and comics – much of it concerning animals, weirdos and people who get left out. You can see her drawings on her blog at **www.everyoneisherealready.blogspot.com**. You can email her at **everyoneisherealready@gmail.com**.

Simon Barraclough hails from Yorkshire and now lives in London. He won the poetry section of the London Writers' Prize in 2000 and his 2008 debut *Los Alamos Mon Amour* (Salt Publishing, 2008) was shortlisted for Best First Collection in the Forward Prizes. His work has appeared in *Poetry Review*, *The Guardian*, *Magma* and the *FT* and he regular contributes to BBC Radio 3 and 4. **www.simonbarraclough.com**

Julia Bird grew up in Gloucestershire and now lives in London, where she work as a literature promoter, through her company Jaybird. *Hannah and the Monk* is her first poetry collection (Salt, 2008).
http://juliabird.wordpress.com

Niall Campbell is 25 and comes from the Western Isles of Scotland. He graduated from the MLitt in Creative Writing at St Andrews University with distinction in 2009 and has had several poems published, most notably in the magazines *The Literateur* and *The Red Wheelbarrow*. He is currently working towards his debut pamphlet.

Michael Chance is a young artist and illustrator based in Manchester. Currently he designs *Fatzine*, a platform for young musicians, writers and artists, as well as designing gig posters and taking as many illustration commissions as he can find! His personal work as an artist is informed by postmodern philosophical principles and Taoist philosophy, and looks towards the natural world as a place for simplicity, clarity and moral centredness. He enjoys using a mixture of drawing, painting and print-making techniques rooted in figurative drawing skills, whilst taking an experimental approach. **www.mjfchance.co.uk**

Tom Chivers is a writer, editor and live literature producer, currently living in London's East End. His books include *How To Build A City* (Salt, 2009) and, as editor, the anthologies *Generation Txt* and *City State: New London Poetry* (Penned in the Margins, 2006 & 2009). His pamphlet *The Terrors* (Nine Arches Press, 2009) was shortlisted for the Michael Marks Award. Tom is is editor-in-chief of online literary review *Hand + Star* and director of Penned in the Margins, as well as being co-director of the London Word Festival.
www.pennedinthemargins.co.uk

Hanna Terese Christiansson was born in 1981 in Stockholm. She graduated from Central Saint Martin's College of Art and Design in 2009 with a BA in Fine Art. Before her move to London, she studied painting at Pernby's School of Painting, as well as Art History at Stockholm University. After having spent a total of 13 years abroad, she is now based in Stockholm, where she continues to paint. Her work is largely based on Julia Kristeva's notion of the abject, feminism, psychoanalysis and the human form.
www.htchristiansson.com

Monika Cilmi was born in Italy and has studied art ever since. She has a BA in Visual Arts and a PG in Asian Art, and she has just completed an MA in Fine Art with a project on nature and gesture through the expression of calligraphy. She works as a lecturer and tutor and has had exhibitions in Germany, Italy and England, as well as winning prizes for her work. Her artworks are inspired by her own nature and her relationship with the Earth. She has a passion for Japanese art and aims to express natural energy, harmony and movement through the use of line and mark. **www.monikacilmi.com**

John Clegg is studying for a PhD in Durham. Some of his poems are published in *Succour*, *Magma*, *The Rialto* and *Pomegranate*. His pamphlet, *Advancer*, is available online at **www.silkwormsink.com/chapbook_17.html**.

Dave Coates is 24, was born in Belfast and lives in Edinburgh. He recently co-edited an anthology of poems tangentially related to the World Cup 2010, with Forest Publications. If he ever gets a tattoo it will be of a heron.

Phil Cooper is an artist/illustrator/designer who lives and works in Norwich. He loves comics and disco and books. See more of his work at **www.petitmal.co.uk** and **http://philcooperpetitmal.blogspot.com**.

Balancing the blade's precision with free-flowing designs, **Lois Cordelia** cuts spirited paper 'silhouettes' using a scalpel. Born in 1982 in Ipswich, Lois is a self-taught artist. Since graduating from Edinburgh University in 2006 with an Honours degree in Arabic, she has renewed her focus on the visual arts through exhibiting in a series of solo and joint shows in the UK and Germany. Her website features work in a diverse range of media and styles: silhouette paper-cuts, portraits in acrylics and pastels, wildlife art, still-lifes, Arabic calligraphic composition, and sculpture. **www.loiscordelia.com**

Lorna Crabbe graduated with a BA (Hons) in Fine Art, and the Graduate Certificate in Book Arts, and works primarily with drawing, painting, artists' books, and lino printing. More recently she has branched into illustration. Her work addresses hoarding, the homemade, women and craft history, ornithology and accidental collections. Lorna works from her studio by the sea in Hastings, where she organises exhibition projects and events, and organises the annual Coastal Currents arts festival. More examples of her work can be found on her website at **www.lornacrabbe.co.uk** and her blog **http://lornacrabbe.blogspot.com**.

Caroline Crew recently graduated from the University of St Andrews, and is headed to Emory, Atlanta on the Bobby Jones Scholarship. She likes baking, ales, mushroom foraging and offensive cross stitch. Her work has recently appeared in *Anon 7*. You can read her posts about poetry at **www.carolinemarycrew.wordpress.com**.

Nia Davies writes fiction and poetry. In 2008 she was awarded a place on the Welsh Academi Mentoring scheme for writers. She was born in Sheffield and lives in London. Nia is web editor for *Literature Across Frontiers*. **http://niadavies.wordpress.com**

Lizzy Dening is a freelance journalist specialising in wildlife. Her poetry has appeared in *The Rialto*, *The Times*, *Orbis*, *Rising* and *Pomegranate*. **www.lizzydening.co.uk**

Isobel Dixon's latest collection is *A Fold in the Map* (Salt, 2007), and her next, *The Tempest Prognosticator*, will be published by Salt in July 2011. Not much of a twitcher, she misses the birds of her native South Africa and is glad some pop by these isles occasionally. Find out more online at **www.isobeldixon.com**.

Philip Elbourne is an artist living and working in the North-West of England. His work includes painting, sculpture, photography and illustration, and can be seen at **www.philipelbourne.blogspot.com**.

Dai George's poetry has appeared in *Magma* and *Inscape*. Until recently a masters student in New York, he has also spent time in Wales and now lives and writes in London.

Matthew Gregory was born in Suffolk and studied at the Norwich School of Art and Design and Goldsmiths, University of London. He has lived in Prague, St Petersburg and New York, and won an Eric Gregory award for his work in 2010.

Cliff Hammett is a new media meddler and creative all-rounder. Recent projects have included experimenting with the use of text messaging networks to support sex work activism, an aborted attempt to subvert anti-benefit thief advertising and distributing books from fictitious libraries to park-goers in Southend-on-Sea. He likes to find time for a poem now and then.

Aiko Harman is a Los Angeles native now living in Scotland, where she earned an MSc in Creative Writing from the University of Edinburgh. She has also lived in Japan, teaching English to high school students and spending time with her maternal family. Aiko's poems are published in *Anon, Edinburgh Review* and *The Human Genre Project*, among others. **www.lionandsloth.com**

Emily Hasler was born in Felixstowe but has escaped. She works at Down House, the home of Charles Darwin. Her poems have appeared in publications including *Poetry Salzburg, Horizon Review, The Rialto* and *Warwick Review*. In 2009 she came second in the International Edwin Morgan Poetry Competition. Her favourite bird is a spangled cotinga, though she has only seen one dead in a case.

Holly Hopkins grew up in Ascot and now lives in London. She won the Foyle Young Poets of the Year Award twice and has been published in *Poetry Review* and *The Rialto*. She has also written articles for *Poetry News* and *Poetry International Web*.

Nicholas Hughes trained at Chelsea School of Art. His drawings, book designs and paintings can be found at **http://diddletron.com**.

i-lib *(I lurk in bushes)* translates Edwardian style imagery into surreal and dreamlike visions of anthropomorphic subjects and their relationships to love, hate, life, death and each other. His fine and delicate lines in the drawings, mechanical and interactive sculpture-animals and installations made of lifeless objects lead us into an extraordinarily lively poetic world. **http://ilurkinbushes.co.uk**

Kirsten Irving is half of the team behind Sidekick Books and cult handmade poetry and arts magazine *Fuselit*. She released a pseudonymous collaborative pamphlet with Jon Stone through Forest Publications in 2010, called *No, Robot, No!* **www.drfulminare.com**

Andrew Jamison was born in Co. Down in 1986. His poetry has appeared in *Poetry Review, Poetry Ireland Review 100, The Rialto, The Yellow Nib, The Ulster Tatler* and *The Dark Horse*, with poems forthcoming in *The Moth, The SHOp* and *The Red Wheelbarrow*. In 2009, he was awarded a General Arts Award from the Northern Ireland Arts Council, and was selected for Poetry Ireland Introductions.

Amy Key grew up in Kent and Tyneside and now lives and works in London. Her poetry has been published in *Magma*, *South Bank Poetry*, *Smiths Knoll*, *Rising* and the anthology *City State: New London Poetry* (Penned in the Margins, 2009). Her debut pamphlet, *Instead of Stars*, is available from tall-lighthouse.

Judith Lal was born in the Cotswolds in 1975. She has an MA in Creative Writing from UEA and received an Eric Gregory Award in 2001. Her poems have been published in various magazines, including *Poetry London*, *Poetry News*, *The Rialto*, *Ambit*, *Magma*, *Mslexia*, *The North* and *Aesthetica*. Her pamphlet, *Flageolets at the Bazaar* (Smith/Doorstop, 2006) was chosen as a Poetry Book Society Recommendation.

Alexandra Lazar is a freelance artist and writer and the art editor of *Chroma*. Her drawings are published and exhibited internationally. She has curated several exhibitions and collaborative drawing projects, and is currently completing her research on ideological and value mechanisms in the art of Eastern Europe.
www.cyanworks.com

Natalie Lazarus is a London based artist and illustrator. Alongside her own practice she has also worked within the contemporary art world since graduating with a Fine Art degree 10 years ago, namely for the London gallery White Cube, artists Jake and Dinos Chapman, and, most recently, Cerith Wyn Evans. For more information about her work, please visit **www.natalielazarus.co.uk**.

Katherine Leedale describes herself as 'a photography student, trying to improve.' You can see more of her artwork on her website **www.katherineleedale.com** and her blog **toomanydinosaurs.blogspot.com**.

Roddy Lumsden was born in St Andrews and lives in London. His latest collection, *Third Wish Wasted*, was published in 2009 and his anthology *Identity Parade: New British and Irish Poets* is available now from Bloodaxe. His next collection, *Terrific Melancholy*, will be out in mid-2011, also from Bloodaxe.

Edward Mackay lives and writes in London. His online poetry collection is titled *Postcards from Doggerland*. Find out more at **www.edwardmackay.com**.

Marion McCready studied Politics, Classics and Philosophy at Glasgow University and in 2003 won the RSAMD Edwin Morgan Poetry Prize. Her poetry has appeared in a variety of publications including *Poetry Scotland*, *The Edinburgh Review*, *The Glasgow Herald* and *Horizon Review*. Calder Wood Press will be publishing a pamphlet of her poems in 2011. She also occasionally plays the guitar.

Siofra McSherry was born in Northern Ireland. She studies and teaches American Literature at King's College London and is a freelance journalist and art critic. She lives in Dalston.

Matt Merritt is originally from Leicestershire and studied History at Newcastle University. His pamphlet, *Making the Most of the Light*, was published by HappenStance in 2005 and his collection, *Troy Town*, was published by Arrowhead Press in 2008. He is currently working with photographer Tom Bailey on *Goosepastures*, a collection about Captain Pouch and the Midlands Revolt of 1607. Matt works as the features editor at *Bird Watching* magazine and is co-editor of *Poets On Fire*, as well as blogging at **http://polyolbion.blogspot.com**.

Kate Parkinson was born in 1985. She studied Fine Art and Art History at Lancaster University, and, upon graduating, was selected for the Northern Graduates degree show at the Curwen Gallery, London. Now working in publishing, but still creating work in own time, Kate is available for further commissions on **kateparkinson100@hotmail.com**.

Saroj Patel is a London based illustrator and artist. She posses a unique, distinctive style and produces elaborate illustrations of animals and nature. Her work is both conceptual and abstract and displays a fluidity of movement through the use of lines and patterns. She uses bold and bright colours to bring her work to life, mainly through the medium of acrylic and ink. You can see more of her work at **www.sarojpatel.com**.

Kate Potts lives in London and is about to begin a PhD on radio verse drama at Royal Holloway. Her pamphlet, *Whichever Music* (tall-lighthouse, 2008) was a PBS Choice and was shortlisted for the Michael Marks Awards. Her work also features in the anthology *Voice Recognition: 21 Poets for the 21st Century* (Bloodaxe, 2009). In 2009 she received an Arts Council grant to assist with her first full-length collection, which is due for release in 2011 from Bloodaxe.

Richard Price's latest poetry collection is *Rays* (Carcanet, 2009). His recently-published novel, *The Island* (Two Ravens, 2010), follows a father and a daughter who steal a car as an act of revenge.
www.hydrohotel.net

Fiona Purves graduated from Edinburgh College of Art in 2009 with a degree in Illustration. She is influenced by the spontaneity of observed drawing, alongside the peculiar personalities found in animals. These inform an instinctive approach to drawing, which explores the character of her subject. She is working towards a children's book full of animals. Her favourite things besides drawing include baking, dogs and 80s films. See more of her work at **fionapurves.co.uk**.

Declan Ryan was born in Mayo, Eire in 1983 and lives in North London, where he works as a freelance writer. He programmes and hosts poetry and prose night Days of Roses and recently co-edited an anthology of 12 poets who have read at the series. His poems have been published in, or are forthcoming from, *Bedford Square IV* (John Murray) and *The Rialto*. Dec is also the singer in The Shingles.
www.myspace.com/theshinglesband

Bethany Settle lives in Norwich, where she works in the Millennium Library, and is currently writing her first novel.

Jon Stone was born in Derby and currently lives in Whitechapel, London. He is co-creator of arts magazine Fuselit, as well as one of the editors at Sidekick Books. Jon's first pamphlet, *Scarecrows*, was published by Happenstance Press in 2010. His chapbook of comic book poetry, *Thra-koom*, was published online later in the same year, and is available from **www.silkwormsink.com/chapbook_25.htm**.

Jennie Webber is a freelance illustrator, based in London. With a passion for natural history and a fondness for oddity and intrigue, her drawings explore the gap between fact and fiction, often concealing hidden treats for the viewer along the way. She favours large-scale wall installations and builds the structure of her drawings with patterns that are half-invented, half-derived from texture. Using recycled paper and sustainable art materials, Jennie Webber upholds an ethical art practice. See more on her website **www.jenniewebber.com** and blog **www.jenniewebs.blogspot.com**, or contact her at **jennie@jenniewebber.com**.

James Wilkes's most recent poetry collection, *Weather A System*, was published by Penned in the Margins in 2009. Recent pamphlets include *Reviews* (Veer, 2009) and *Conversations After Dark* (Sideline Publications, 2010). He regularly collaborates with visual artists, and is studying for a PhD at the London Consortium, where he is writing about the landscape of the Isle of Purbeck in Dorset.
www.renscombepress.co.uk

Chrissy Williams lives in London and has had poems published in *S/S/Y/K/4*, *The Rialto*, *Dial 174*, *Orphan Leaf Review*, *Fuselit*, *Rising*, *Southbank Poetry* and *The Rialto*. She works at the Poetry Library and wishes she had a dog. Chrissy's chapbook, *The Jam Trap*, is available for free on **www.silkwormsink.com/chapbook_19.html**, and her blog can be found at **chrissywilliams.blogspot.com**.

About
Sidekick Books

Sidekick Books is based in London, UK, and publishes collaborative collections of poetry and illustration at the behest of head editor (and excommunicated alchemist) Dr Fulminare and his evil familiar, Bandijcat.

For a full list of publications please visit **www.drfulminare.com**.